the very busy writer

copyright © 2024
all rights reserved

The Very Busy Writer

written by Emma Fulenwider
illustrated by Marci Seither

One morning,

a story made friends

with a special sort of person

"**BING**!" said the school notification app, "*We're short on volunteers today!*"

"**BUZZ BUZZ**" went the smart watch,

"*You haven't stood up in an hour, it's time to move!*"

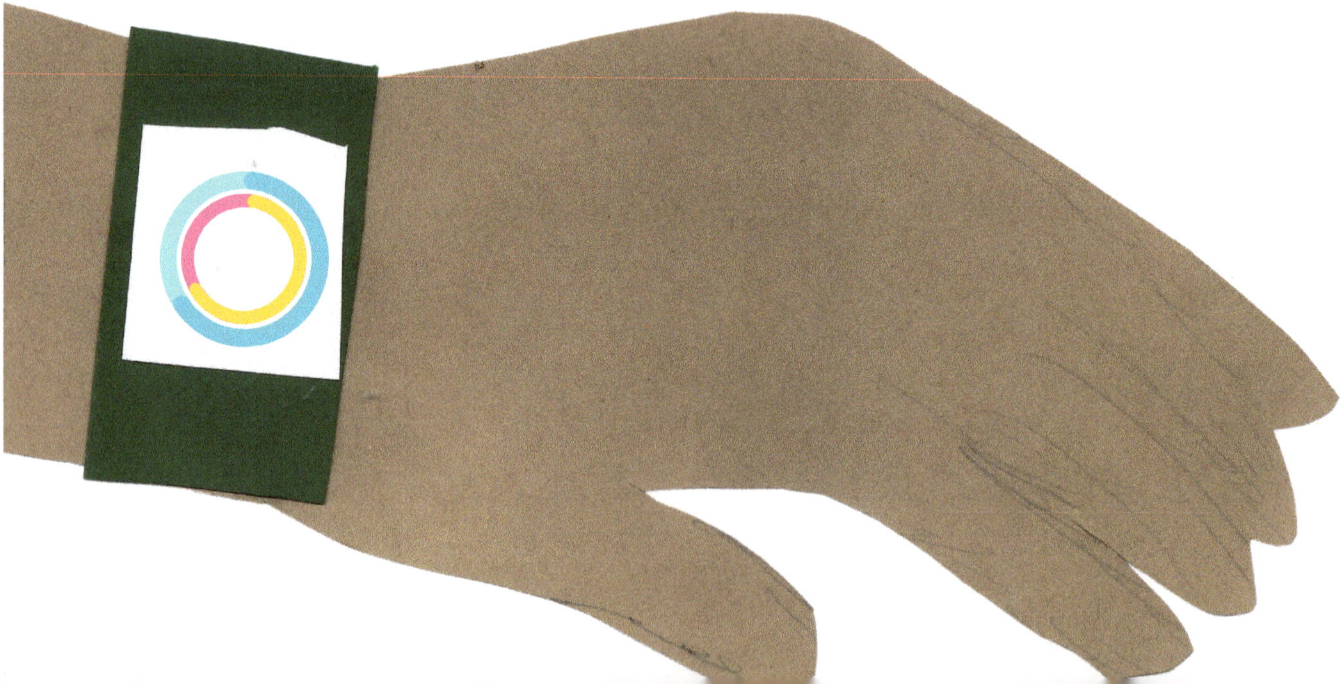

The writer didn't answer. They were very busy writing their book.

"**BRRRR**," said the coffee,

"*Why don't you reheat me and have a little snack.*"

The writer didn't answer. They were very busy writing their book.

"**HEYYYYY!**" said the work email,

"*Can you finish this project over the weekend?*"

The writer didn't answer.
They were very busy
writing their book.

"**BEEP BOOP**" said the remote,

"*A new season of your show just dropped!*"

The writer didn't answer. They were very busy writing their book.

"**LETS GO!**" said the basketball,

"*Tryouts are today!*"

The writer didn't answer. They were very busy writing their book.

The writer didn't answer.
They were very busy
writing their book.

"BUILD YOUR PLATFORM!" said the experts,

"You need a newsletter"

"and a podcast"

"and a website"

NOW

"*Pssst,*" whispered the new story idea,

"*why don't you write me instead?*"

The writer didn't answer...

"*Excuse me,*" said the book,

"*aren't you going to write my ending?*"

the end

About

Marci Seither and Emma Fulenwider are a mother-daughter duo who have attended writer's conferences together for 25 years.

Marci is a contributor to Guideposts and WORLD Magazine who lives in Knoxville, Tennessee. Emma is a literary agent who lives in Sacramento, California.

This book may have been a distraction from their writing.

www.ingramcontent.com/pod-product-compliance
Lightning Source LLC
LaVergne TN
LVHW072123060526
838201LV00068B/4959